Name: Sir Thomas More, English statesman
Prison: Tower of London, England 1534–1535
Crime: treason

Name: Antonio Cassatta, Italian merchant
Prison: Doge's Prison, Venice 1609–1628
Crime: plotting against the Doge

Name: Henrico Mattioli, "The Man in the Iron Mask"
Prison: Bastille, France 1702–1706
Crime: spying

Name: Abel Magwitch*
Prison: prison hulk, England 1820s
Crime: using stolen banknotes
*The convict in Charles Dickens' novel *Great Expectations*

Name: Catherine Reniers
Prison: model prison, Belgium 1876–1882
Crime: fraud and kidnapping

·ROGUES' GALLERY·

Name: Captain Alfred Dreyfus, French army officer
Prison: Devil's Island, French Guiana 1895–1899
Crime: selling military secrets

Name: Josef Stalin, ruler of Russia (1929–1953)
Prison: Siberia, Russia 1913–1917
Crime: planning a revolution

Name: Al "Scarface" Capone, gangster
Prison: Alcatraz 1934–1936
Crime: non-payment of taxes

Name: Douglas Bader, British fighter pilot
Prison: Stalag Luft III, Germany 1941–1945
Crime: prisoner of war

Find these famous prisoners inside this book.

Explore each of their prisons. . . if you dare!

PETER KENT

◆

GO TO JAIL!

A Look at Prisons
Through the Ages

◆

The Millbrook Press
Brookfield, Connecticut

Published in the United States in 1998 by
The Millbrook Press, Inc.
2 Old New Milford Road
Brookfield, Connecticut 06804

First published in Great Britain in 1997 by
Macdonald Young Books, an imprint of
Wayland Publishers Ltd
61 Western Road
Hove, East Sussex BN3 1JD

Commissioning Editor: Fiona Courtenay-Thompson
Editor: Lisa Edwards
Designer: Sally Downes
Illustrator: Peter Kent

Library of Congress Cataloging-in-Publication Data
Kent, Peter.
    Go to jail! : a look at prisons through the ages / Peter Kent.
       p.   cm.
    Summary: Surveys various prisons throughout time, including the
Tower of London, the Bastille, and Alcatraz. Includes brief
biographies and illustrations of nine famous prisoners and
challenges the reader to find them in the larger illustrations.
    ISBN 0-7613-0402-9 (lib. bdg.)
    1. Prisons—History—Juvenile literature.   2. Prisoners—History—
Juvenile literature.   [1. Prisons—History.   2. Prisoners—
History.]   I. Kent, Peter.   Behind bars.   II. Title.
HV8501.K46   1998   97-31893
365', 09—dc21   CIP
                                          AC

Printed by Wing King Tong, Hong Kong

5 4 3 2 1

CONTENTS

◆ INTRODUCTION ◆

There has always been crime, and there has always been punishment. But the idea of keeping someone in prison as a punishment is quite new. For most of history, prisons throughout the world were used only for holding people until they were tried by a court of law. The penalty for a crime was usually the payment of a fine, mutilation, banishment, or death. Up until the late eighteenth century, imprisonment itself was not considered to be a punishment, although it was often a dreadful experience.

The first prisons were generally small and very unpleasant. Jailers were often lazy and inefficient and many prisoners died of disease. Prisoners were kept together in cells—only the most important people got their own rooms. Up until the late nineteenth century, there was no system of grading and separating the different types of criminals. Young children in prison for their first crime were locked up with violent thieves and murderers.

The idea of long prison sentences began in the nineteenth century. It was no longer possible to send criminals abroad to penal colonies (see page 20) and the death penalty was reserved for murderers only. The number of inmates began to rise dramatically. Prison reformers began to complain about how dirty and cruel prisons were. They said that prisons made criminals worse. Prisons had to be clean, healthy, and fairly run. Inmates needed their own cells and should be given useful work to do. Many governments followed these suggestions as they set up new prison systems.

Today, prison overcrowding remains a problem all over the world, and people still campaign for better conditions for inmates.

◆THE INCARCERATED CAST◆

Most of the prisons in history have held a range of characters with a great deal in common. There have been nice and nasty jailers—although, of course, just how nasty they were has varied enormously. You will also find that different types of convicts coped with their imprisonment in remarkably similar ways. There were always prisoners who kept trying to escape, and there were always those who tried to make the best of it by obtaining all the comforts they could. Every prison had at least one inmate who would not obey the rules, and there were always those who, however fair the jailers, were miserable.

In every prison in this book, you will find these five characters. Look carefully; the "incarcerated cast" may be dressed very differently. . . .

The governor or
head jailer

The kind jailer

The prisoner who has
made himself comfortable

The prisoner obsessed with trying to escape

The cruel jailer

In each of the prisons in this book there is also a famous prisoner. Find out about all of them in the Rogues' Gallery and spot them if you can.

In addition, you must find the prisoner's pet. There is one in each picture. Some prisoners were allowed to keep dogs and cats in prison, while others made do with birds, rats, mice, spiders, and cockroaches. These creatures did not provide much companionship, but were better than nothing during long years of loneliness in a cell.

THE TOWER OF LONDON ◆1534◆

The Tower of London was built by William the Conqueror, king of England, soon after 1066. It was designed as a fortress but it eventually became a prison. The Tower was not a jail for ordinary criminals—noblemen and people who had offended the king were kept there. Three queens had their heads chopped off inside the Tower, two kings were murdered there, and many famous people were executed on the hill outside its walls. The list of famous prisoners is long: from Anne Boleyn, the second wife of King Henry VIII, to Rudolf Hess, the deputy leader of Nazi Germany.

Most prisoners arrived by barge through a watergate on the Thames River. This became known as Traitors' Gate. The prisoners were important people and were usually kept in quite comfortable conditions. But there was one horrible cell called Little Ease. It was only 4 feet (1.2 meters) square and the prisoner inside could neither stand, sit, nor lie down. The Tower had no torture chamber but a rack was kept there and often used.

The Tower was not just a gloomy prison. It was used to store weapons, armor, and the crown jewels; some of these can be seen there today. At one time, all of England's money was made at the Tower in the royal mint. The king once had a private zoo there as well. It housed a lion, an elephant, and a polar bear which fished in the Thames River.

The Tower was used as a prison again in both World Wars. Eleven spies were shot there during World War I (1914–1918).

THE DOGE'S PRISON ◆1620◆

For hundreds of years, the ruler of the city of Venice in northern Italy was known as the Doge. His palace was one of the

most beautiful buildings in the world but it was attached to a dark and gloomy jail called the Prison Palace. Most of the inmates were thieves and murderers, but there were also a few special prisoners. These were people who disagreed with the Doge and they were often sent to prison without a trial. The only evidence of such a "crime" was an unsigned letter sent to the Doge by a neighbor. Anybody could write to the Doge in secret using special mailboxes around Venice.

After they had been sentenced, prisoners were led from the Doge's palace over a bridge to the jail. For many of them, it was their last look at the outside world and the bridge became known as the "Bridge of Sighs."

THE BASTILLE ◆ 1700 ◆

The Bastille in Paris was the most infamous jail in France. Mysterious legends were told about the inmates who were taken there secretly, in closed coaches, by order of the king. Most were noblemen accused of plotting against the king and were held for years without trial. Actual conditions inside were not as grim as as everyone liked to believe. The prisoners, to whom the jailers never spoke, were reasonably well treated—*if* they behaved well.

On July 14, 1789, the Bastille was captured by the citizens of Paris. They opened all the cells but found only seven prisoners: Four were forgers and three were insane. The storming of the Bastille was the start of the French Revolution and the day is still a national holiday in France.

◆A PRISON HULK◆1820◆

In 1776 all of the jails in England were full. No more convicts could be squeezed in. To solve the problem, two old warships were moored on the Thames River near London as floating prisons, or hulks. About 250 men were kept on each ship. They wore brown uniforms and heavy leg irons. Every day, they went ashore to work on building sites.

By 1820 there were over a dozen hulks. Life on board was hard and grim; it was always cold and damp. The warders were brutal, the food was disgusting, and bullying and fighting amongst the prisoners went on all the time. The hulks were very unhealthy and one in four of the prisoners died. These horrible floating jails were used until 1857, when new prisons were built on land with plenty of room for all of the convicts.

The idea of prison hulks has been revived. Because of a shortage of land in New York City, the prison authority could not enlarge the existing jails or build new ones. So, in 1993, they bought a floating prison. The *Vernon C. Bain* is nearly 700 feet (200 meters) long, weighs around 20,000 tons, and holds 800 prisoners. In 1997 British jails were so crowded that a new prison ship was towed from America and moored in Portland Harbor. Hulks were back in business.

◆A MODEL PRISON◆1880◆

This picture is based on one of the model prisons that was built in the nineteenth century. Each prisoner had their own cell. The blocks of cells were arranged like a star so that each could be watched by the guards in the middle. There were separate cell blocks for men and women, although most prisons held men only. These new prisons were designed to be clean, healthy places where the criminal learned to regret his crime and become a better person.

Many new jails used the "separate system." The prisoners were not allowed to speak to one another for fear they would swap criminal ideas. They worked hard, either on a treadmill or alone in their cells.

Prisons like this one held three hundred inmates. The prisoners exercised alone in separate pens. In the chapel they sat in boxes, unable to see each other. Many prisoners were very miserable and some of them went insane.

◆ DEVIL'S ISLAND ◆1897◆

Imagine being sent not to a prison, but to a strange, wild country halfway across the world as punishment: a hot, often unhealthy place where you would spend lonely years—perhaps the rest of your life—thousands of miles from home.

During the eighteenth and nineteenth centuries, European countries often punished people by sending them to overseas settlements called penal colonies. England shipped many people to Australia, while France set up colonies in Africa and South America. The most feared French colony was Devil's Island, which was about 6 miles (10 kilometers) from the coast of French Guiana in South America. The very worst convicts, guilty of the most terrible crimes, were sent there.

Devil's island had first been used as a hospital for people ill with leprosy. In 1895, it was turned into a prison. About 1,200 convicts and 150 wardens lived on the island. The island, only 1.2 square miles (2 square kilometers) in size, was surrounded by rocks, rough seas—and sharks. The sharks were said to be the best guards and only one prisoner is thought to have escaped in over 40 years.

French penal colonies were abolished in 1938, but Devil's Island remained a prison until 1958. It is now in ruins and overgrown by a thick rain forest.

♦SIBERIA♦1910♦

The dreary wastes of Siberia, in northeastern Russia, made a vast, natural prison from which it was almost impossible to escape. The climate was harsh—it was freezing cold in winter and baking hot in summer. Life there was very hard and unpleasant.

The Tsars (rulers) of Russia began sending criminals to Siberia in 1648.

In the 1700s they started to send people who disagreed with the government (political exiles). Then they sent peasants who disobeyed their landlords, and finally those who failed to pay their taxes. Most criminals lived in labor camps and were made to work, often in gold mines. Political exiles were allowed to earn their own living if they wanted to. Just to be in Siberia was punishment enough for them.

Most of the political exiles lived in small, remote villages hundreds of miles from the nearest town. They rented their own houses, where they could do what they liked. The police kept a careful eye on them, but it was the long distances and awful climate that prevented them from escaping.

Even so, the exiles went on plotting against the rule of the Tsars. They managed to spread their ideas of revolution by writing to their friends, even though letters took months to arrive. Nearly all the leaders of the 1917 Russian Revolution had spent a few lonely years in Siberia.

◆ALCATRAZ◆1936◆

lcatraz was the most famous and feared prison in the United States. It stands on a rocky island in San Francisco Bay, California. Alcatraz became a prison for the most dangerous and desperate convicts in 1933. Conditions were tough on "The Rock," which was usually surrounded by thick, cold, wet fog. About three hundred convicts were kept in three blocks of cells. All one hundred wardens had rifles and machine guns, and there were tear gas sprinklers fixed to the dining room ceiling in case of rioting.

n the thirty years it was operating, it is thought that no one successfully escaped from Alcatraz. Five prisoners are still missing, possibly drowned in the bay. No executions were held at Alcatraz but there were five suicides and eight murders!

The prison was finally closed in 1963. *Alcatraz* means "pelican island" in Spanish, but there are no pelicans or prisoners there now—only lots of tourists.

◆ STALAG LUFT ◆ 1943 ◆

During wartime, millions of men and women are put in prison without committing a crime. They are called prisoners of war. During World War II (1939–1945), both German and Allied armies kept large numbers of their enemies prisoner until the fighting ended. Over 150,000 British servicemen were captured by Germany.

A set of strict rules drawn up at the Geneva Convention stated how prisoners of war were to be treated. They had to be kept in a safe place away from the fighting. They had to have shelter, enough food, and proper medical care. Most prisoners were kept in specially built camps of wooden huts surrounded by high barbed-wire fences.

Many prisoners of war spent their time planning to escape. They forged identity cards and made civilian clothes out of uniforms, blankets, and pieces of curtain.

This prison camp was one of several that were built to hold Allied airmen whose planes had been shot down over Germany. These camps were called *Stalag Luft*, meaning "air prison," because they were run by the German airforce. About three hundred men were confined to one camp.

There were about fifty guards—mostly middle-aged men who were not fit enough to fight.

In all, there were hundreds of escapes from the Stalag Luft camps, but very few men actually managed to reach home.

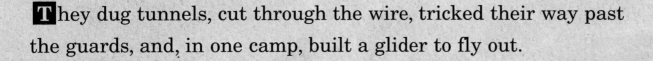

They dug tunnels, cut through the wire, tricked their way past the guards, and, in one camp, built a glider to fly out.

◆ PECULIAR PRISONS ◆

Some very odd places have been used as prisons. Some of these prisons will seem very peculiar if your idea of a prison is a large building with bars in the windows.

◀ Criminals in the Italian city of Mantua were displayed to the people in an iron cage. The cage was fixed to a tower nearly 100 feet (30 meters) above the ground.

▲ This hole in the ground with bars made of logs is a village prison in Java, Indonesia.

◀ A hollow tree trunk fitted with bars once made a snug little jail for a Slovakian village. As many as six prisoners could be squashed inside.

A fourteenth-century German bishop had a ▲ cell in the spire of his cathedral. The prisoners were deafened by the ringing of the bells.

◀ In 1760, an Italian artist named Piranesi published a book of drawings called *Imaginary Prisons*. The pictures were gloomy and terrible. Eighteenth-century architects were very influenced by Piranesi and built real prisons to look like his imaginary ones.

▲ In 431 B.C. a great army from Athens in Greece was defeated by the Spartans in Sicily. The survivors were kept prisoner in an old quarry. Many of them died there.

▲ Pugachev led an unsuccessful peasant revolt against Catherine the Great, who was the Empress of Russia from 1773 to 1775. As punishment, he was driven around the country in an iron cage. After several months he was taken to the city of Moscow and executed.

▲ Anthony Grey, a British journalist in Beijing, China, was imprisoned on the top floor of his house by Chinese Red Guards from 1967 to 1969. They did this because some Chinese journalists had been sent to prison in Hong Kong, which was then under British rule.

◀ The empty cages in Antwerp Zoo in the Netherlands were used to hold German soldiers captured by Allied armies in 1944. The animals had all died of starvation.

Name: Sir Thomas More, English statesman
Prison: Tower of London, England 1534–1535
Crime: treason

Name: Antonio Cassatta, Italian merchant
Prison: Doge's Prison, Venice 1609–1628
Crime: plotting against the Doge

Name: Henrico Mattioli, "The Man in the Iron Mask"
Prison: Bastille, France 1702–1706
Crime: spying

Name: Abel Magwitch*
Prison: prison hulk, England 1820s
Crime: using stolen banknotes
*The convict in Charles Dickens' novel *Great Expectations*

Name: Catherine Reniers
Prison: model prison, Belgium 1876–1882
Crime: fraud and kidnapping

·ROGUES' GALLERY·

Name: Captain Alfred Dreyfus, French army officer
Prison: Devil's Island, French Guiana 1895–1899
Crime: selling military secrets

Name: Josef Stalin, ruler of Russia (1929–1953)
Prison: Siberia, Russia 1913–1917
Crime: planning a revolution

Name: Al "Scarface" Capone, gangster
Prison: Alcatraz 1934–1936
Crime: non-payment of taxes

Name: Douglas Bader, British fighter pilot
Prison: Stalag Luft III, Germany 1941–1945
Crime: prisoner of war

*Find these famous
prisoners inside
this book.*

*Explore each of
their prisons. . .
if you dare!*